She always knew how to brighten my day, as well as others...

She worked so hard every day...

Whenever she started laughing, I would laugh with her...

I could always count on her to put a smile on my face...

She could always do her makeup even when driving...

Her kind heart and radiant smile were such a blessing...

Carlie had the biggest heart, a wild but genuine personality...

Her laughter was super contagious...

Everyone should look up to her...

She was always encouraging others...

She always would say hi and smile...

I wouldn't be who I am without her...

She taught me to always be happy and kind to everyone...

Her heart was so big and full of gold...

She laughed and smiled unlike anyone else...

Carlie made me a better person; it's always good to have people around you that bring you closer to God...

I will always miss her but I know she's watching over me until we meet again...

The Carlie Challenge

-Attitude of Gratitude-

#thecarliechallenge

The Carlie Challenge

By Carlie Almond

ISBN -13: 978-154671767

(CreateSpace)

Sometimes
ALL YOU NEED
to do is
STOP
and realize all the
blessings
GOD
has given you.
♡ - Carlie Almond

INTRODUCTION

"Who are we?"
"The Almonds!"
"Why?"
"Because we love each other!"

The Almond family used this chant in their living room to incite enthusiasm or lift each other up when life just seemed a little bumpy. They had no idea that chant would be the last words they shared with their 15-year-old daughter and sister, Carlie, as she was taken off life support.

It is often said when a death occurs the one who dies is in a better place but the ones left behind on Earth are those left with the grief and the pain. What a remarkable life it is to know that Carlie Almond left her loved ones with a legacy of joy, gratefulness, and peace that somehow starts to fill the hole she left behind.

Carlie was just like most other teenagers in the Midwest. She loved her family, participated in sports, cherished her friends, and looked forward to a wide open future. She also experienced typical emotions like fear, jealousy, loneliness, and the other millions of thoughts that spark in the brain of teenagers.

That's why in late December 2015 when she developed a nasty cold and was diagnosed with bronchitis, there was no cause for alarm. She embraced her days of Christmas vacation by watching movies, texting friends, and adding in a few extra minutes of sleep to her day. She also remained dedicated to her basketball practices and it wasn't until the last day of practice on New Year's Eve that she had to cut out early from exhaustion and had a friend take her home.

One drive home, a quick once-over from her mother Amy, several phone calls, and a trip to the local ER is all it took for everything to change. The normalcy that Carlie brought to her family was turned on its head. Doctors and nurses in the emergency room, many of whom knew Carlie and her family, raced to keep her breathing but their efforts simply could not stop the pulmonary embolism that coursed through her veins. With her parents, Brad and Amy, and younger brother Garrett surrounding her bed, the tubes were removed, and Carlie took her last breath on this Earth as they repeated the familiar chant:

"Who are we?"
"The Almonds!"
"Why?"
"Because we love each other!"

In a small town like Chanute, Kansas, you know your neighbors. You share their joy and feel their pain. The news of Carlie's death spread quickly and a blanket of grief was cast upon the small community. The world around Chanute lost its color and the sun didn't shine as brightly as before.

A week later 1,400 people filled the high school gymnasium to embrace each other, cry on each other's shoulders, and make some attempt at celebrating the life of Carlie.

As the community attempted to return to some sense of normalcy without her in it, a former hometown girl was wandering through Carlie's Facebook page and found a challenge Carlie had given herself shortly before her death. Just two months earlier, she spent time each day creating a post of someone or something for which she was grateful. This is an exercise practiced in many forms all over social media, but Carlie didn't know that her own posts would lead to a life-changing challenge in such a short time.

An online challenge was organized in Carlie's name for Facebook followers to continue her attitude of gratitude, which eventually led to #thecarliechallenge. The social media challenge spread like wildfire and in a short time, more than 3 million people had taken #thecarliechallenge. To this day, reflections of gratitude can be seen on social media with that same hashtag, allowing Carlie to continue to impact this world.

Several years before her death, Carlie went to church camp with a local group. She looked forward to the things that all kids do at camp: swimming, games, hanging out with friends, and of course, freedom from parents. But she was in for a life-changing week and called home to tell her parents that she had given her life to God and was choosing to live her life as a Christian. What came from this young girl for the next several years was a glimpse of God. She had a sparkle in her eye and a zeal for life. She was overwhelmed by God's love.

While Carlie can no longer speak to the reader of this book for herself, the words she left behind can. The actions she demonstrated in her hometown continue to speak her name. And her love for God can be experienced by every reader of these pages.

Read "The Carlie Challenge" with an attitude of gratitude. While you think of her life and the impact she has left on the world, also think about your own life and the things that make you thankful. Even in a season of pain and despair, light can be found in the things we take for granted. Carlie was a light in the darkness and continues to shine today. Allow her words to help guide you to that light.

#thecarliechallenge

The following pages will lead you through Carlie Almond's daily thankfulness challenge that she completed in November of 2015. The adjacent page to each post is a place for reflection on your own life. Lines are provided for you to journal your own thoughts, write names of people who have influenced you, and create your own gratitude list.

Enjoy soaking up the words of Carlie day by day and allow her to speak to you through these pages.

Carlie Almond

November 2, 2015 ·

Well I'm a day late but I want to join in on the day of thanks. So for yesterday, I am thankful for my parents, Amy Almond and my dad Brad. They are both my rocks. They are two of the greatest people I will ever know. I hope someday to be half the parents they are to me and my brother. They support me in everything I do and are always there to brighten my day by making me smile. I wouldn't be where I am today without them. I love you both forever and ever. 🖤❤

Day 1 Challenge

Family is usually at the top of the list when anybody is asked what they are thankful for. Your "family" may not look like Carlie's. Families today are made up of many different people, different backgrounds, and different dynamics. But we all know that person or people who helped shape us into who we are. Who are you grateful for that you consider your family? Who is it that makes you smile by thinking of their presence in your life? Reach out to them today and tell them how thankful you are for their influence in your life.

_____

_____

_____

_____

_____

_____

_____

_____

_____

_____

_____

_____

_____

_____

_____

_____

_____

_____

_____

Today, I am thankful for my grandparents.. Beverly McGee and my grandpa Mike, Phyllis Almond and my grandpa John. I just wanted to tell you guys how thankful I am to have such amazing grandparents that come to as many events as they can to support me and my brother, you love and care for us with all your heart, and continually telling us stories that we will cherish for a lifetime. Also for giving us such great advice on life. I am forever thankful to have such amazing grandparents like you. I love you 😊

Day 2 Challenge

Grandparents were not only influential to Carlie, but they were also present for many of the activities in her life. She mentions the stories that they shared with her in her Day 2 post. Those stories created an image for her to lovingly remember the lives of her grandparents, but they also helped add shape to her future. Who shares stories with you that draw you in and begin to impact your decisions? Tell that person how much you love to hear the stories and be grateful when those stories influence your decision-making in the future.

_____

_____

_____

_____

_____

_____

_____

_____

_____

_____

_____

_____

_____

_____

_____

_____

_____

_____

<u>Carlie Almond</u>

November 3, 2015 ·

Best Friends.
Today I am thankful for the great advice giving and supportive friends that I am blessed with. In every situation they give off a positive attitude and continually making me laugh. I couldn't live without you! I love you guys to the moon and back😊 <u>Keeley Tallent</u>,<u>Kaitlyn Newton</u>n, Lexy, Ashlyn Smoot, and <u>Dannah Hartwig</u> Thank you so much for everything you do for me. Also thanks for the memories we have made and the ones in the making🤍❤

Day 3 Challenge

Friendships should be built on gratefulness for each other. We share our laughter, our pain, our joys, our weaknesses, and our love. Some people have address books filled to the brim with friends while others are lucky to name one or two people who are their best friends. The quantity of our friendships doesn't matter but the depth of our gratitude for each other is where it counts. Who are some friends who you rely on for advice? Who do you seek when you're wanting a good laugh? Tell them today exactly what you see in them that makes a good friend. Don't let the day go by without telling them how much they mean to you.

_____

_____

_____

_____

_____

_____

_____

_____

_____

_____

_____

_____

_____

_____

_____

_____

_____

_____

Carlie Almond

November 4, 2015 ·

Day 4
I am thankful for not only being blessed with a great family and friends, but I am also just thankful for anyone that has impacted my life. I am forever thankful for you and the many positive things you have added to my life. Also to the man upstairs for granting me with all of these awesome things to be thankful for.

Day 4 Challenge

There's an old church hymn that says, "Count your blessings, name them one by one..." There are times when blessings seem scarce. Friends have let us down. Family brings stress and drama. Work and school seem pointless and never-ending. But we are reminded today to simply be thankful for the ability to be thankful. We can all name one blessing, from the roofs over our heads to the ones sitting next to us. From there count your blessings and find joy in how they begin to pile up.

_____

_____

_____

_____

_____

_____

_____

_____

_____

_____

_____

_____

_____

_____

_____

_____

_____

_____

_____

Carlie Almond

November 5, 2015 ·

Day 5
Today I am thankful for being able to be active again after the long road that is finally behind me. Tearing my ACL has definitely been one of the best and worst things to happen to me. Why did this happen to me, crossed my mind a lot I'm not gonna lie. But on the flip side..It has taught me a lot about being strong, believing in myself and also being thankful that it wasn't worse. I have connected with so many more people than I ever would have if I wouldn't have gotten hurt. I have learned about the awesome support team we have in our school and in my life. I am super thankful to be back. Thank you to everyone for the encouraging words and pushing me to better myself🖤❤

Day 5 Challenge

Most people will see the inside of an ER, operating room, or at least see a doctor for something that seems life-altering. Car wrecks, falls, muscle tears, and broken bones are a part of life and while they are inconvenient and uncomfortable, a fast recovery is often dependent upon a positive attitude. A smile on your face to the nurse or a simple "thank you" to the doctor sets the tone for your care. And while you may be the one in need of medical care, remember that a positive and gracious spirit may be the healing medicine needed by someone else you encounter.

_____

_____

_____

_____

_____

_____

_____

_____

_____

_____

_____

_____

_____

_____

_____

_____

_____

_____

Carlie Almond

November 6, 2015 ·

Day 6
Kurt Umbarger. From being one of my dads closest friends to being one of the most inspirational people I know. You are a hero. I may not see you everyday or even at all lately, but your strong courage and heart you have given since your accident has made me realize what an awesome person you are. You may have had some rough times in the past but who hasn't?? By the way I am so proud of you and the person you have fought to be. Anyways.. with your awesome personality and determination you can conquer anything. I just wanted to tell you that you have always been there for me and pushing me to be a better person and always making me smile with your not so funny jokes, lol. I am forever thankful for that. What breaks you down can only make you stronger.. Love you always♥❤ thanks for adding value to my life☺

Day 6 Challenge

At some point in life we have all known or met someone we marvel at who has faced a life-changing event. We wonder how the inspirational speaker we just heard survived a plane crash with such a positive outlook, even while in a wheelchair. We are astounded at a friend battling cancer and still finding the time to be concerned about others. These trials in life will come down our own paths at some point and in different circumstances. With an attitude of gratitude, others will marvel at your spirit as well. Who are some of the people who have inspired you? What ways did they turn the corner in a bad situation to make it better? How can you apply that to even the simplest situation in your own life?

_____

_____

_____

_____

_____

_____

_____

_____

_____

_____

_____

_____

_____

_____

_____

_____

_____

_____

Carlie Almond
November 7, 2015 ·

Day 7
Today I am thankful for having such great role models in my life.
Family, Friends, Teachers.. etc. LOTS of you have impacted my
life in a positive way and have helped shape the person I am. I
have been blessed to learn from some of the greatest people
around. Thank you! ♥❤

Day 7 Challenge

"Family, friends, teachers, etc..." These are the people Carlie listed who had a positive impact on her life. But more importantly, these people likely demonstrated unconditional love for her. Even in our bad moments of yelling, throwing a fit, and slamming doors, there are some people who love us through those times. Who has loved you unconditionally? What is in their character that makes them love you no matter what?

_____
_____
_____
_____
_____
_____
_____
_____
_____
_____
_____
_____
_____
_____
_____
_____
_____
_____
_____
_____

Carlie Almond

November 8, 2015 ·

Day 8
Today I am thankful for the beautiful fall weather God has blessed us with 🖤💙🍂

Day 8 Challenge

The environment around us can set the tone for a good day or a bad day. Some people like the hot summertime, others soak up the cool breeze of fall, and there are some who count the days until the first snowfall and cold temperatures. Carlie found peace in the fall weather and gave thanks to the one who created it. Look around yourself right now. What sets the tone for the environment you are in that makes it comfortable? Sometimes finding simple things like a cool room on a hot day, a candle burning to make your room smell good, or the perfect lighting that welcomes you home are where we should find our gratitude. Name some of those things that surround you to make life better.

_____

_____

_____

_____

_____

_____

_____

_____

_____

_____

_____

_____

_____

_____

_____

_____

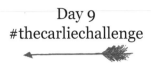

Carlie Almond

November 9, 2015 ·

Day 9
Today I am thankful for my past. Everything thing that has
happened to me good and bad has brought me to who I am today.
I couldn't be more thankful for what I have and what my past has
taught me😊🤍❤

Day 9 Challenge

The past...for many people the past holds unpleasant memories. We want to push those experiences far back into our minds and forget them. However, our past creates the person we are today and how we live tomorrow. Even bad memories and life experiences are in place and can be used for good. Pain creates healing, chaos creates peace, and sadness creates joy. Think of the things in your past that have made you who you are today, good or bad. What are some of the bad things in your past that have made you a better person today? What are the good things that can help you set the tone for tomorrow?

_____

_____

_____

_____

_____

_____

_____

_____

_____

_____

_____

_____

_____

_____

_____

_____

_____

_____

_____

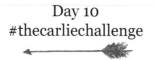

Carlie Almond

November 10, 2015 ·

Day 10
Today I am thankful for all of my aunts. Carrie Hegg Sarah
Steinman and Jamie Craig are super awesome people that have
brought lots of love and laughter into my life. Thank you for being
the best aunts around💜❤

Day 10 Challenge

Carlie was blessed with a loving relationship with her mother, but she also recognized her aunts as women who provided her with the same type of motherly love and fun she experienced with her own mom. We all have women who have influenced our lives, given us a shoulder to cry on, or made us laugh until we cry. In a world where the role of women can be lost in our boundless society, we need to honor those women who offer their knowledge and love. Name three women who have had a significant impact on your life. Text or call them today to tell them how important they are to you and to your future.

_____

_____

_____

_____

_____

_____

_____

_____

_____

_____

_____

_____

_____

_____

_____

_____

_____

_____

Carlie Almond

November 11, 2015 ·

Day 11 💚❤

Today I am thankful to all of you that have served and to the ones that are still serving our country. I am forever thankful for your service and your dedication to our country. I am also thankful for a special veteran, my uncle <u>Waylon Steinman</u>. You worked super hard to serve our country and I am forever proud of you and your accomplishments. Thank you for all you have done for our country and for me 😊🇺🇸

Day 11 Challenge

It doesn't take long to watch the cable news channel and see war and devastation across the world. Most readers of this book have drawn the lucky card to be born into a country where we have almost infinite freedoms, due to the dedication of military men and women who have fought to establish those freedoms. Think of a family member or friend who has served, no matter how long ago or how long their duty. Tell them how thankful you are to be doing something as simple as reading this book because of their dedication.

_____

_____

_____

_____

_____

_____

_____

_____

_____

_____

_____

_____

_____

_____

_____

_____

_____

_____

Carlie Almond

November 12, 2015 ·

Day 12
Today I'm thankful for Sydney Trout. Your going through something super rough right now that was similar to the same thing I went through.. You have such an up-beat spirit and you never fail to make me laugh. I know lately that you feel as if things aren't in your favor with the surgery in all, but it will all eventually be okay😊 I can only hope and pray that things go in your favor throughout recovery. Your a super strong girl. With lots of great things going for you. This is a set back I know for sure, but I know you can push through & better yourself. Also you'll come back even stronger. You've got this! Thank you so much for being a great friend for anything and everything. Love you syd💜❤💜❤

Day 12 Challenge

Hearing the words of Carlie's friends, it is evident that she was an encourager. They relied on her for her uplifting spirit and words of confidence. Sometimes the only thing a friend needs to hear is, "You've got this!" Who can you reach out to today who needs uplifting? Who is struggling that you can help?

_____

_____

_____

_____

_____

_____

_____

_____

_____

_____

_____

_____

_____

_____

_____

_____

_____

_____

_____

_____

_____

Carlie Almond added 2 new photos.

November 13, 2015 ·

Day 13
Today I am thankful for not only an amazing best friend, but being able to experience the opening KU game with my family and Ashlynn. 😊 #rcjh 💜💜❤

Day 13 Challenge

Sometimes the things we find to be thankful for aren't necessarily people but instead, the things we experience. Carlie was a University of Kansas Jayhawks fan and loved the experience she had at the season opening game that fall. Maybe you have a favorite team, or favorite band, or maybe even favorite books that bring you joy and let you experience life at a different level. It's okay to express your gratitude even for things that seem out of the norm.

_____

_____

_____

_____

_____

_____

_____

_____

_____

_____

_____

_____

_____

_____

_____

_____

_____

_____

_____

_____

Carlie Almond

November 15, 2015 ·

Day 14
Today I am thankful for both my mom Amy Almond and dad for pushing me to always be the best I can be. Also especially lately for helping me build myself up for the turkey trot. Another person is Beth Bell for always being so encouraging and for being such a sweet blessing in my life. Your awesome! Thank you guys♥❤♥❤ ♥❤

Day 14 Challenge

Even though the life of Carlie could seem pretty flawless, you can bet she had the same anxieties and pressures any teenager faces. She wanted to fit in without compromising who she was. She faced nervousness and fear just like anybody else. What anxieties have you faced that you conquered? Who helped you face those fears? How did it help you to conquer a challenge?

_____

_____

_____

_____

_____

_____

_____

_____

_____

_____

_____

_____

_____

_____

_____

_____

_____

_____

_____

_____

Carlie Almond with Amy Almond and 5 others.
November 15, 2015 ·

Day 15
Today I am more than thankful for my family. Yesterday and today I got to spend time with some of my family! They always have kept me laughing. I couldn't ask for a better family to support me and encourage me. I am forever blessed to have you all💚💜💚💜 thank you guys for being there for me and being such fun people to be around! Family time is by far the best time. I love you guys to the moon 😊

Day 15 Challenge

Usually when we think of being thankful, it is for other things. But have you ever thought of being thankful for yourself? Yes, gratitude is something given to others, but you can also look in the mirror and be thankful for simply being you. You have been created in such a manner that makes you unique. The joys in life, combined with the heartaches, have resulted in your personality. The DNA your parents gave you has determined the special quirks in your design that make you special. Be thankful today that you are special, unique, and that you are simply you.

_____

_____

_____

_____

_____

_____

_____

_____

_____

_____

_____

_____

_____

_____

_____

_____

_____

Day 16
#thecarliechallenge

Carlie Almond with Shannon Bogle and 13 others.
November 16, 2015 ·

Day 16
I am thankful for my basketball family. Each one of you are so
encouraging to others and are constantly pushing yourself to do
better! Thank you for being such fun and hard working people to
be around that help me improve and push myself each day to be
better player and person! Thank you 🖤

Day 16 Challenge

We tend to surround ourselves with like-minded people. You may be a musician, a car racer, a baseball fanatic, or a book reader. Those special attributes in our character shape our social circles. Think about your social circles and how they have benefitted your life. How do you contribute to help benefit others in that circle, too? Are there any social circles in your life that are not healthy for you?

_____

_____

_____

_____

_____

_____

_____

_____

_____

_____

_____

_____

_____

_____

_____

_____

_____

_____

Day 17
#thecarliechallenge

Carlie Almond with Amy Almond and 5 others.
November 18, 2015 ·

Day 17
I am forever thankful for my moms Shear Class workers
throughout all the years. From being the Guinea Pig on all of the
new products or equipment to the many laughs and tears.. I have
loved looking up to such beautiful and talented people. I wouldn't
trade growing up around all of you guys for anything. Thank you
for always taking me in as your own and always being such sweet
and awesome people to be around! Love you guys bunches😊
missing my girl Delfina more than ever. Never forgotten💜❤

Day 17 Challenge

When you were born, you came into this world with a purpose. It probably won't be revealed to you through a miraculous sign. Nor will anybody come to you and tell you what your purpose is. But as you live your days, you will shape that purpose and begin to use it to impact the world. You may be a friend to the friendless, an open door to the lonely, a table of food for the hungry, or even just a friendly smile for others. Take time to examine yourself and what you have to offer. Stretch yourself and find ways to give your abilities to those around you.

_____

_____

_____

_____

_____

_____

_____

_____

_____

_____

_____

_____

_____

_____

_____

_____

_____

_____

_____

Carlie Almond

November 18, 2015 ·

Day 18
Today I am thankful for my best friend Keeley Tallent. I just
wanted to put it out there how thankful I am for you and all you
do for me. We have gotten so much closer this year. From
knowing each other through day care days to now we have made
some super awesome memories😊 You have always been my go to
and my bestfriend and someone that makes life so much better!
Don't know what I would do without you! Thank you for being
you and being such a strong inspiration in my life! 💜❤💜❤

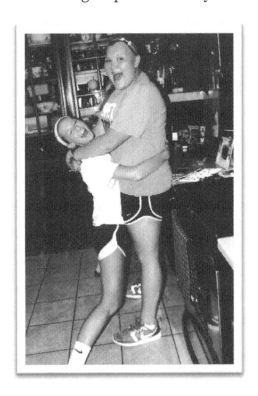

Day 18 Challenge

Life is made up of small moments. They pass by quickly and seem insignificant. But they begin to pile up, piecing together the quilt pattern that is your life. Those moments keep you going when you want to give up, put a smile on your face even when you're alone, and they begin to overflow to others. Be thankful for the little moments and remember that the mountain they are creating is more significant than the big moments.

_____
_____
_____
_____
_____
_____
_____
_____
_____
_____
_____
_____
_____
_____
_____
_____
_____
_____
_____
_____
_____

Carlie Almond

November 19, 2015 ·

Day 19
Today I am thankful for my goofy and fun loving brother! Family is everything and he definitely makes it special! Don't know what I would do without him! Love you forever and always bub♥❤♥
❤ Amy Almond

Day 19 Challenge

Carlie's brother Garrett has been left with a heart full of memories with her, from toddler snuggles to wrestling on the living room floor as he grew older. Her love for him as a big sister is reflected in who he is becoming today. Reflect on those who had the same impact on your childhood, whether it is a sibling, a cousin, or even a best friend. What memories do you have that you know helped create your character today?

_____

_____

_____

_____

_____

_____

_____

_____

_____

_____

_____

_____

_____

_____

_____

_____

_____

_____

_____

_____

_____

Carlie Almond

November 20, 2015 ·

Day 20
Today I am thankful for Gods grace. I wouldn't be where I am today without the love God has given and shown me. I am forever thankful for his love and hope he gives me day in and day out. All of these thankful things I have found to be thankful for in my life would not be possible without the lord. I am thankful to be a Christian. ♥❤

Day 20 Challenge

Carlie unashamedly lived her life as a Christian. Her love for God and passion for doing his work was evident in her words and actions. Consider your own spiritual life, whether it comes from a background of strong faith or maybe just a church visit with a grandparent once in a while. Think of the prayers said for you or the prayers you have said on your own and how those have changed your course. Reflect on the spiritual nature of your life.

_____

_____

_____

_____

_____

_____

_____

_____

_____

_____

_____

_____

_____

_____

_____

_____

_____

_____

_____

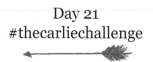

Carlie Almond with <u>Jill Kepley</u>.
November 21, 2015 ·

Day 21
Today I am thankful to be able to watch 3 of the cutest little kids ever. Every time I come over they make my day so much better😊 I have had so much fun getting to know them and watch them grow over the last few years! Thank you for being such precious kids! p.s I didn't get a pic of Ty but he is just as sweet and adorable believe me🖤❤

Day 21 Challenge

Little children bring a smile to the faces of most people, whether it is a cute photo online or a happy baby in our arms. Even if you don't have children of your own, there are kids around you who bring you joy. No matter their age and understanding, be sure to tell them how much they mean to you and what their life does to improve your own.

_____

_____

_____

_____

_____

_____

_____

_____

_____

_____

_____

_____

_____

_____

_____

_____

_____

_____

_____

Day 22
#thecarliechallenge

Carlie Almond with Phyllis Almond and Beverly McGee.
November 23, 2015 ·

Day 22
I am thankful for the sweetest grandparents ever who do so much for me and my brother 😊

Day 22 Challenge

At this point in the challenge, Carlie has used words like joy, laugh, smile, thankful, value, family, inspirational, and more. What word best describes the way you've spent the last month of your life?

_____

_____

_____

_____

_____

_____

_____

_____

_____

_____

_____

_____

_____

_____

_____

_____

_____

_____

_____

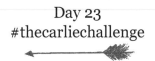

Day 23
#thecarliechallenge

Carlie Almond with <u>Amy Almond</u>.

November 23, 2015 ·

Day 23
I am thankful that my parents returned safely and had such a great time celebrating turning 40 in New Orleans! missed them bunches! Love you! super glad your home🖤❤

Day 23 Challenge

In a world of Instagram, Snapchat, and other social media sites centered around photography, it is hard not to get wrapped up in the lives of others. We look at vacation photos, family pictures, friends getting together, and begin to compare those against our own lives. But we have to remember that those photos are one simple, staged glimpse of their lives. We all have our great moments but we also all have our down times. When those feelings of jealousy begin to enter your mind, turn your thoughts to the things around you that bring you joy, that bring you life, and that can't always be captured in an Instagram photo.

_____

_____

_____

_____

_____

_____

_____

_____

_____

_____

_____

_____

_____

_____

_____

_____

_____

_____

Carlie Almond
November 26, 2015 ·

Day 24
I am thankful for my fun loving great-grandma😊 she loves and
cares for everyone she meets! Don't know what we would do with
out you nanny🖤❤ I love you bunches and I am super thankful to
have such an amazing nanny!

Day 24 Challenge

Carlie's great-grandma held a special place in her heart even with their decades of age difference. In her great-grandmother's 90 years of life, she has lived through highs and lows of experiences that many will not. At the age of her great-grandma, what things do you think will matter to you the most? Family? Friends? Fun? Finances? Are the things you hold important today going to continue to be important as you age?

_____

_____

_____

_____

_____

_____

_____

_____

_____

_____

_____

_____

_____

_____

_____

_____

_____

_____

Day 25
#thecarliechallenge

Carlie Almond with Sarah Steinman and 2 others.
November 26, 2015 ·

Day 25
I am thankful for all of my cousins! They have all brought so much joy into my life! I love you all with all my heart! 🖤❤ I couldn't ask for a better family with amazing cousins😊

Day 25 Challenge

Contentment and gratitude are not the same thing, but they are closely related. How many times are we given something and then realize there is more to be had? We only want more from that point on, rather than being thankful for what we have. Gratitude is the art of knowing what we have is enough. Name three people you know who need to be prayed for. Send them a card telling them you have been thinking of them and praying for them.

_____

_____

_____

_____

_____

_____

_____

_____

_____

_____

_____

_____

_____

_____

_____

_____

_____

_____

Carlie Almond with <u>Amy Almond</u>.
November 27, 2015 ·

Combing day 26 and 27 because it means too much to me to just make it one day♥❤
The holiday season has already started off great! Lots of shopping and spending time with family at thanksgiving. I am beyond blessed and thankful to have an amazing close family, great friends who continue to make life even better. I am surrounded by amazing people and I couldn't be more thankful to have each one of you in my life😊 thank you for adding so much fun and value to my life♥❤ forever thankful for all of you!! ♥❤♥❤

Day 26 Challenge

We all have expectations, whether it is knowing you'll have a pair of new tennis shoes under the Christmas tree or maybe you can count on an envelope of cash from Grandma. During your next holiday season, put away the expectations and focus on appreciating what you have and the people who have given that to you. Help others during the season and find that happiness grows where gratitude is planted. Are there any serving opportunities in your area that are open on Thanksgiving or Christmas? Pick one and serve at one this year!

_____

_____

_____

_____

_____

_____

_____

_____

_____

_____

_____

_____

_____

_____

_____

_____

_____

_____

Day 27
#thecarliechallenge

Day 27 Challenge

Use today to pay it forward. Write down several ways you can randomly extend gratitude to a stranger. Invite friends to join you in this challenge.

_____

_____

_____

_____

_____

_____

_____

_____

_____

_____

_____

_____

_____

_____

_____

_____

_____

_____

_____

_____

_____

_____

_____

Carlie Almond added 3 new photos — with Amy Almond.
November 28, 2015 ·

Day 28
Today I am extra thankful for my amazing mom! You have taught me so much in my life already! Your someone I look up to every single day! Thank you for being such an amazing mom! I am blessed to have you in my life. Thank you for all you do for me and everyone else! I love you with all my heart! I hope you have had an amazing day💚❤ I can't wait to spend many more birthdays with you! HAPPY 40th mom😘💃

Day 28 Challenge

When you think about the people in your life who have given you love and support, what qualities do they have to make you want to spend time with them, know them more, and be like them? List those qualities that are most attractive to you. How can you implement those characteristics into your own life?

_____

_____

_____

_____

_____

_____

_____

_____

_____

_____

_____

_____

_____

_____

_____

_____

_____

_____

_____

_____

_____

Carlie Almond

November 29, 2015 ·

Day 29
Today I am thankful for <u>Dannah Hartwig</u>💚❤ I hope you have had a great birthday! Thank you for the continuous laughter and support in everything! Love you girl😊 HBD🎉

Day 29 Challenge

As The Carlie Challenge wraps up in this book, it is time for you to turn the spotlight toward yourself and determine ways to give to the world around you. One famous quote says, "Feeling gratitude and not expressing it is like wrapping a present and not giving it." You have that present. It is wrapped in the finest paper of gratitude. Share it with the world. Is there someone that you are close with who needs encouragement?

_____

_____

_____

_____

_____

_____

_____

_____

_____

_____

_____

_____

_____

_____

_____

_____

_____

_____

_____

_____

Carlie Almond

November 30, 2015 ·

Day 30
Today I just want to thank all of you for the constant love and support in my life! The month of November has taught me a lot of about being thankful for something new day in and day out! I couldn't be more blessed to live my life surrounded by such awesome and inspirational people! 💚💜 thanks a bunch everyone 😊 you guys all mean a lot to me💚💜💚💜

Day 30 Challenge

You have probably experienced the loss of a loved one. It is a painful and inevitable part of life. Carlie's family and friends would give up this book and the millions of wonderful words shared with them if they could have her back on this Earth. But her sweet smile captured in photos, her words forever etched in this book, and the kind and loving character she was, left an engraving on this world that cannot be erased. Think of your own words and actions today and how you can heal the past, make the best of today, and impact the future.

_____

_____

_____

_____

_____

_____

_____

_____

_____

_____

_____

_____

_____

_____

_____

_____

_____

_____

Dear Reader,

The Carlie Challenge doesn't end here. The readers of this book have the opportunity to write the next chapter. You are challenged to continue the spirit of thankfulness in everything you do, 24/7. That means in time of happiness, be thankful. In times of loneliness, be thankful. In times of grief, be thankful.

Carlie demonstrated that no matter what you are facing in life, you can have an attitude of gratitude. She even found gratitude during the healing pain of ACL surgery, opening day of University of Kansas basketball, and babysitting the little kids of a friend.

It is time for you to take this opportunity and no longer live your life with "me first." Share this challenge with others and invite them to join you on this journey. And even if you are fearful of how to pray or what to say, simply telling God that you are thankful for everything He has done is the first step. Then you will be taken deeper into the challenge of living a grateful life for Him.

You don't have to live a celebrity lifestyle to have an impact on others. Money, fame and popularity only give a false impression of what you can do in the world. Carlie was a normal, midwestern teenager, yet her influence is significant on the hearts of millions who never even met her. She wrote these first pages of The Carlie Challenge, now it is up to you to turn the page and continue with the next chapter.

Pastor D.J. Dangerfield
(Carlie's youth pastor and mentor)

ACKNOWLEDGEMENTS

Carlie's story is continuing with the efforts of so many friends and family who have worked to keep her memory alive. Special contributors were Robynn Coates, D.J. Dangerfield, Lila Hulse Dunning, Shanna Foster Guiot, Ragan Vogel, Dustin Fox, Stacy Henson, and Jenny Diveley. Their dedication to this work is a testament to the impact Carlie had on those around her.
We also want to thank everyone who has shared their love, prayers, and support, which continue to this day. We love you!

Brad, Amy, and Garrett Almond